IN THE STOPPING TRAIN

DONALD DAVIE

IN THE STOPPING TRAIN
& other poems

New York
Oxford University Press
1980

FOR DOREEN

Acknowledgements:

Certain of these poems have appeared in the following periodicals: *Agenda, Critical Quarterly, Delta, English, The Listener, The London Magazine, Encounter, The New Statesman, Poetry Nation, Poetry Nation Review, The Times Literary Supplement*. 'Horae Canonicae' was read over the air for a programme of the B.B.C. Thanks are due to the editors of these magazines, and of that programme, for permitting these poems to be reprinted.

First published in Great Britain by
Carcanet New Press Limited, 1977

Library of Congress Cataloging in Publication Data
Davie, Donald
In the stopping train & other poems

I. Title.
PR6007.A66715   1980   821'.9'14   79-16688

ISBN 0-19-520175-2

Printed in Great Britain

CONTENTS

FATHER, THE CAVALIER

I have a photograph here
    In California where
You never were, of yourself
    Riding a white horse. And
The horse and you are dead
    Years ago, although
Still you are more alive
    To me than anyone living.

As for the horse: an ugly
    Wall-eyed brute, apparently
Biddable enough, for I cannot
    Believe you were ever much of
A horseman. That all came late:
    Suddenly, in your forties,
Learning to ride! A surrogate
    Virility, perhaps . . .

For me to think so could not
    Make you any more
Alive than you have been here,
    Open-necked cricket-shirt
And narrow head, behind
    The pricked ungainly ears
Of your white steed—all these
    Years, unnoticed mostly.

THE HARROW

Unimaginable beings—
Our own dead friends, the dead
Notabilities, mourned and mourning,
Hallam and Tennyson . . . is it
Our loss of them that harrows?

Or is it not rather
Our loss of images for them?
The continued being of Claude
Simpson can be imagined,
We cannot imagine its mode.

Us too in this He harrows. It is not
Only on Easter Saturday
That it is harrowing
To think of Mother dead,
To think, and not to imagine.

He descended into—
Not into Hell but
Into the field of the dead
Where He roughs them up like a tractor
Dragging its tray of links.

Up and down the field, a tender bruising,
A rolling rug of iron, for the dead
Them also, the Virtuous Pagans
And others, He came, He comes
On Easter Saturday and

Not only then He comes
Harrowing them—that they,
In case they doubted it, may
Quicken and in more
Than our stale memories stir.

THE DEPARTED

They see his face!

Live in the light of . . .

Such shadows as they must
cast, sharp-edged;
the whole floor, said to be crystal,
barry with them. And long!

Spokes that reach even to us,
pinned as we are to the rim.

ROUSSEAU IN HIS DAY

So many nights the solitary lamp had burned;
So many nights his lone mind, slowing down
Deliberately, had questioned, as it turned
Mooning upon its drying stem, what arc
Over a lifetime day had moved him through.

Always he hoped he might deserve a Plutarch,
Not to be one posterity forgot.
Nor have we. He has left his mark: one tight
Inched-around circuit of the screw of light,
As glowing shadows track the life of roses
Over unchosen soil-crumbs. It was not
What he'd expected or the world supposes.

AFTER THE CALAMITOUS CONVOY (JULY 1942)

An island cast
its shadow across
the water. Where
they sat upon
the Arctic shore
it shadowed them.

The mainland rose
tawny before
their eyes and closed
round them in capes
the island must
have slid from, once.

Under one horn
of land not quite
naked, above
the anchorage
white masonry
massed round a square.

From there one gained
the waterfront
by, they perceived,
a wooden stair
that wound down through
workshops and godowns.

Admiringly
their eyes explored
make-do-and-mend:
arrangements that
the earth lent—stairs,
cabins on struts,

stages of raised
catwalks between
stair and railed stair,

staked angles, ramps
and landings in
the open air.

Roof of the world,
not ceiling. One
hung to it not
as flies do but
as steeplejacks
move over rungs.

Survivors off
the Russian run,
years later they
believed the one
stable terrain
that Arctic one.

DEPRAVITY: TWO SERMONS

(1) Americans: for their Bicentennial

The best, who could, went back—because they nursed
A need to find depravity less dispersed,
Less, as it seemed, diluted by crass hope.
So back went Henry James to evil Europe,
Unjust, unequal, cruel. Localized,
The universal could be realized
In words and not in words; not by the Press
Nor the theatrical Pulpit. Prefaces
Delineate the exquisite pains he took
To bottle up a bad smell in a book.
Inordinate pains! For Paris, London, Rome
Were not much less disorderly than back home;
There too, already, what he sought was traced
Upon no maps, but must be found by Taste,
A nostril lifted to the tainted gale
Of words, of words—all shop-soiled, all for sale.
Each year that he survived, things fell apart
Till H. G. Wells was 'Life', and he was 'Art'.
'Life'! Is it something else than life, to live
On the scent always of that faint, pervasive
Smell that alone explains what we've become?
What ought to be, and once was, axiom?

(2) St Paul's Revisited

'The change of Philomel, by the barbarous king,
So rudely forced'.
(In the myth, Philomela became a nightin-
gale, and Tereus, her ravisher, a hoopoe.)

Anger, a white wing? No, a hoopoe's wing,
King Tereus, Hatred. Crested ravisher,
The motley lapwing whoops and whoops it up
Greek Street and Fleet Street till the gutters run
Their serial feature. Liquid, yellow, thick,
It pools here, fed from the Antipodes,
The Antilles . . . For the seven seas run with bile
To the Pool of London, sink where the ordure, talent
At home in this world, gathers. And it pools
Not only there but in whatever head
Recalls with rage the choir of Christ and Wren.

Horned and self-soiling, not the barbarous king
Of Thrace and the anthologies, nor a brute,
A plain quick killer, but degenerate,
The rapist lapwings sideways through our heads
And finds no exit. There's a place it might:
The A-to-Z preserves no record of it
Though Strype or any antique gazetteer
Describes it well enough, a Thames-side borough
Decayed already, called Depravity.
If we could find it now, our hoopoes might
Hop from inside our heads, and Thames run cleaner.

Anger won't do it. Ire! Its hooked bill gouges
The chicken-livers of its young. Irate,
We are depraved, and by that token. Gulls
Cry, and they skeeter on a candid wing
Down slopes of air, but not for anger's sake.
Spite, malice, arrogance and 'Fuck you, Jack',
Birds in the gables of Depravity
Twitter and cheep, but most inside my head
And can be lived with. But the hoopoe whoops
Always inside, and rancorous. Rancour! Rancour!
Oh patriotic and indignant bird!

SEEING HER LEAVE

'gardens bare and Greek'
—Yvor Winters

This West! this ocean! The bare
Beaches, the stony creek
That no human affair
Has soiled . . . Yes, it is Greek,

What she saw as the plane
Lifted from San Jose.
Under the shadow of Wren
She walks her ward today;

Once more my tall young woman
Has nerved herself to abandon
This Greece for the Graeco-Roman
Peristyles of London,

Where the archaic, the heated,
Dishevelled and frantic Greek
Has been planed and bevelled, fitted
To the civic, the moralistic.

And that has been noble, I think,
In her and others. Such
Centuries, sweat, and ink
Spent to achieve that much!

Lloyds of London, some
Indemnity for our daughters!
Those who trust the dome
Of St Paul's to the waters . . .

So much of the price is missed
In the tally of toil, ink, years;
Count, neo-classicist,
The choking back of tears.   *(California)*

MANDELSTAM, ON DANTE

(1)
Russian Jew, for you
   To re-think Dante, dissolve
Into fluids that four-square slab
   Of Christendom, meant a resolve

(So it must seem) to taunt
   And tempt the unsteadied Gentile,
As it might be me, to act
   In nettled Stalin's style.

Dangerous, these corrosives
   You handle. First and last
Powder the graven image!
   'Jew' means 'iconoclast'.

Can we believe the impulse
   Consciously suicidal?
Or was the play of mind
   Lordly, the interest idle?

(2)
About the skies, you went wrong somewhere. Let
Some nearer neighbour of theirs make the corrections.
For them it was easier, them the nine Olympic
Dantescan discuses, to clang directions!

You are not to be thought of apart from the life you lived.
And what Life intends is at once to kill and caress
That thus the distress which beat in on your ears, on your eyes
And the sockets of your eyes, be Florentine.

Let us not then assign to you, no, let us not fit about your
Hollowed-out temples that bittersweet prickle, the laurel—
Better in your case if we should split your
Heart into blue and clamorous bits of ocean.

For when you died, having served out your time,
You in your time friend to all lifetime-livers,
Yes, there transpired a broader, a loftier chime
Sent from the skies in your entire chest's heavings.

(3) *(Voronezh, 1937)*
'About the skies, I went wrong somewhere. Let
Some nearer neighbour of theirs make the corrections.
For you it was easier, you the nine Olympic
Dantescan discuses, to clang directions,
Be out of breath, get black and blue contusions . . .

But Thou, if Thou art not the heretofore's
Nothing-accomplishing hero, if Thou art bent
Standing over me now, wine-steward, to proffer the cup,
Pour me the strong wine, not the ephemeral ferment
To drink of, to pledge the vertiginous, towering, straight-up
Insane blue-azure's hand-to-hand engagement.

Dovecotes, black holes, starlings' nesting-boxes,
Blue of the bluest, case of the key at its keenest,
Ice of the heretofore, high ice!—ice of the Spring . . .
Clouds, look—the clouds, against soft collusions embattled . . .
Quiet now! Storm-clouds, see where they lead them out,
                                        bridled.'

(4)
Rhyme, you once said, only
    Points it up, tags it, the blue
Cabinet-making of Heaven
    And Earth, the elegant joints
All of them flush as given!

Symmetries in this blue
    Cabinet, the small
Rooms of stanzas—in this
    No woe, you said, but the happy
Chances of mathematics.

Clouds come and go like a French
    Polisher's breath on walnut,
Protean, fluid . . . And you
    A lordly squandering playboy!
No bequest but you blue it!

At home in the Empyrean . . .
    Yes, but one joint had sprung
Long, long ago. The woe
    Came, and was Florentine?
As well say: Galilean.

DEATH OF A PAINTER

in memoriam William Partridge

Behind the grid, the radiant
planes and translucent ledges
of colour,

the constructions,

feelingful but extreme
distortions, as my eye found them,

three or four trees and a Norman
church-tower in Leicestershire? Well
yes, if you say so.
You painted always from nature.
That mattered, you always said.

Hard to see why, unless

among these cobalts and
pale yellows, these
increments and crumblings,

in that or another churchyard
we are permitted to speak
to a Divine Distorter
these lines that you occasion.

PORTLAND

after Pasternak

Portland, the Isle of Portland—how I love
Not the place, its name! It is as if
These names were your name, and the cliff, the breaking
Of waves along a reach of tumbled stone
Were a configuration of your own
Firm slopes and curves—your clavicles, your shoulder.
A glimpse of that can set the hallway shaking.

And I am a night sky that is tired of shining,
Tired of its own hard brilliance, and I sink.

Tomorrow morning, grateful, I shall seem
Keen, but be less clear-headed than I think;
A brightness more than clarity will sail
Off lips that vapour formulations, make
Clear sound, full rhyme, and rational order take
Account of a dream, a sighing cry, a moan,

Like foam on all three sides at midnight lighting
Up, far off, a seaward jut of stone.

ORPHEUS

named them
and they danced,
they danced: the rocks, stones, trees.

What had possessed them,
or him? How did it help?

What had got into those stones,
throwing up puffs
of yellow dust as they bounced, and could he
hear them, an irregular percussion
there in the blinding sunlight
like a discotheque at a distance?

No, I'm afraid not; weightless.
For them to dance
they had to be light as air,
as the puff of air that named them.

Thistledown rocks! Who needs them?

Well but, they danced for joy,
his holy joy
in stones, in there being stones
there, that stones should be,
and boulders too, and trees . . .

Is that how it was? One hopes so.

ARS POETICA

*In memoriam
Michael Ayrton,
sculptor.*

Walk quietly around in
A space cleared for the purpose.

Most poems, or the best,
Describe their own birth, and this
Is what they are—a space
Cleared to walk around in.

Their various symmetries are
Guarantees that the space has
Boundaries, and beyond them
The turbulence it was cleared from.

Small clearances, small poems;
Unlikely now the enormous
Louring, resonant spaces
Carved out by a Virgil.

The old man likes to sit
Here, in his black-tiled *loggia*
A patch of sun, and to muse
On Pasternak, Michael Ayrton.

Ayrton, he remembers:
Soon after reading his
Obituary, behold!
A vision of him:

The bearded, heavy-shouldered
London clubman, smiling
Against a *quattrocento*
View of the upper Arno.

This was in answer to prayer:
A pledge, a sufficient solace.
Poor rhyme, and are you there?
Bless Michael with your promise.

The old man likes to look
Out on his tiny *cortile*,
A flask of 'Yosemite Road'
Cheap Chablis at his elbow.   *(California)*

IN THE STOPPING TRAIN

*

I have got into the slow train
again. I made the mistake
knowing what I was doing,
knowing who had to be punished.

I know who has to be punished:
the man going mad inside me;
whether I am fleeing
from him or towards him.

This journey will punish the bastard:
he'll have his flowering gardens
to stare at through the hot window;
words like 'laurel' won't help.

He abhors his fellows,
especially children; let there
not for pity's sake
be a crying child in the carriage.

So much for pity's sake.
The rest for the sake of justice:
torment him with his hatreds
and love of fictions.

The punishing slow pace
punishes also places along the line
for having, some of them, Norman
or Hanoverian stone-work:

his old familiars, his
exclusive prophylactics.
He'll stare his fill at their
emptiness on this journey.

Jonquil is a sweet word.
Is it a flowering bush?
Let him helplessly wonder
for hours if perhaps he's seen it.

Has it a white and yellow
flower, the jonquil? Has it
a perfume? Oh his art could
always pretend it had.

He never needed to see,
not with his art to help him.
He never needed to use his
nose, except for language.

Torment him with his hatreds,
torment him with his false
loves. Torment him with time
that has disclosed their falsehood.

Time, the exquisite torment!
His future is a slow
and stopping train through places
whose names used to have virtue.

*

A stopping train, I thought,
was a train that was going to stop.
Why board it then, in the first place?

Oh no, they explained, it is stopping
and starting, stopping and starting.

How could it, they reasoned gently,
be always stopping unless
also it was always starting?

I saw the logic of that;
grown-ups were good at explaining.

Going to stop was the same
as stopping to go. What madness!
It made a sort of sense, though.

It's not, I explained, that I mind
getting to the end of the line.
Expresses have to do that.

No, they said. We see . . .
But do you? I said. It's not
the last stop that is bad . . .

No, they said, it's the last
start, the little one; yes,
the one that doesn't last.

Well, they said, you'll learn
all about that when you're older.

Of course they learned it first.
Oh naturally, yes.

*

The man in the stopping train
sees them along the highway
with a recklessness like breeding
passing and re-passing:
dormobile, Vauxhall, Volvo.

He is shrieking silently: 'Rabbits!'
He abhors his fellows.
Yet even the meagre arts
of television can
restore them to him sometimes,

when the man in uniform faces
the unrelenting camera
with a bewildered fierceness
beside the burnt-out Simca.

*

What's all this about flowers?
They have an importance he can't
explain, or else their names have.

Spring, he says, 'stirs'. It is what
he has learned to say, he can say
nothing but what he has learned.

And Spring, he knows, means flowers.
Already he observes this.
Some people claim to love them.

Love *them*? Love flowers? Love,
love . . . the word is hopeless:
gratitude, maybe, pity . . .

Pitiful, the flowers.
He turns that around in his head:
what on earth can it mean?

Flowers, it seems, are important.
And he can name them all,
identify hardly any.

*

Judith Wright, Australian

'. . . has become', I said, 'the voice
of her unhappy nation.'
O wistfully I said it.

Unhappier than it knows,
her nation. And though she will tell it,
it cannot understand:

with its terrible future before it,
glaring at its terrible past;

its disequilibrium, its
cancers in bud and growing;

all its enormous sadness
still taking off, still arcing

over the unhistoried
Pacific, humming to Chile.

Stone heads of Easter Island!
Spoiled archipelagos!

How they have suffered already
on Australia's account

and England's. They will suffer
no more on England's.

Judith Wright, Australian,
'has become', I said,

'the voice of her unhappy,
still-to-be-guilty nation.'

Wistfully I said it,
there in the stopping train.

*

The things he has been spared . . .
'Gross egotist!' Why don't
his wife, his daughter, shrill
that in his face?

Love and pity seem
the likeliest explanations;
another occurs to him—
despair too would be quiet.

*

Time and again he gave battle,
furious, mostly effective;
nobody counts the wear
and tear of rebuttal.

Time and again he rose
to the flagrantly offered occasion;
nobody's hanged for a slow
murder by provocation.

Time and again he applauded
the stand he had taken; how much
it mattered, or to what
assize, is not recorded.

Time and again he hardened
his heart and his perceptions;
nobody knows just how
truths turn into deceptions.

Time and again, oh time and
that stopping train!
Who knows when it comes to a stand,
and will not start again?

*

(Son et Lumière)

I have travelled with him many times
now. Already we nod,
we are almost on speaking terms.

Once I thought that he sketched
an apologetic gesture
at what we turned away from.

Apologies won't help him:
his spectacles flared like paired
lamps as he turned his head.

I knew they had been ranging,
paired eyes like mine,
igniting and occluding

coppice and crisp chateau,
thatched corner, spray of leaf,
curved street, a swell of furrows,

where still the irrelevant vales
were flowering, and the still
silver rivers slid west.

*

The dance of words
is a circling prison, thought
the passenger staring through

the hot unmoving pane
of boredom. It is not
thank God a dancing pain,
he thought, though it starts to jig
now. (The train is moving.) 'This',
he thought in rising panic
(Sit down! Sit down!)
'this much I can command,
exclude. Dulled words, keep still!
Be the inadequate, cloddish
despair of me!' No good:
they danced, as the smiling land
fled past the pane, the pun's
galvanized *tarantelle*.

*

'A shared humanity . . .' He
pummels his temples. 'Surely,
surely that means something?'

He knew too few in love,
too few in love.

That sort of foolish beard
masks an uncertain mouth.
And so it proved: he took
some weird girl off to a weird
commune, clutching at youth.

Dear reader, this is not
our chap, but another.
Catch our clean-shaven hero
tied up in such a knot?
A cause of so much bother?

He knew too few in love.

HIS THEMES

(after reading Edmond Jabès)

His themes? Ah yes he had themes.
It was what we all liked about him.
Especially I liked it.
One knew, nearly always one knew
what he was talking about, and he talked
in such a ringing voice.

What did he talk about? What,
just what, were his themes?
Oh, of the most important!

Loss was one of his themes;
he told us, as any bard should,
     the story of our people
     (tribe), he had memorized
     chronologies, genealogies,
     the names and deeds of heroes,
     the succession of our kings,
     our priests, the sept of our pipers,
     the mediations . . . and this
     while, young and old,
     we extolled the immediate, meaning
     the unremembering. *Yes,*
     and what was his theme? His theme, you said, was . . .?
Loss. Loss was his theme.

And duty. He taught us our duty;
he taught us, as any
legislator should,
     the rules of hygiene, the clean
     and the unclean meats, the times and
     the means of fumigation,
     of strewing and spreading, of fires,
     and what to do with the old
     and how to dispose of the dead
     and how to live with our losses

uncomplaining . . . and this
while, young and old,
we did our best to be free,
meaning unruly. *Yes,*
and what was his theme? What did you say his theme
was?

Duty. His theme was duty.

Fear also. Fear was a theme;
he taught us, as all seers must,
continual apprehension:
    of one another, of
    our womenfolk and our
    male children, of
    the next clan over the mountains
    and of the mountains, also
    the waters, the heavenly bodies
    wheeling and colliding,
    of the wild beasts both large
    and infinitesimal, of
    revenants and of the future,
    and of the structure of matter
    and of the unknown . . . and all this
while, young and old,
we tried to keep our nerve,
meaning, to be heedless. *Yes,*
and what was the theme, did you say, of this voice
both hollow and ringing?

Fear. Fear was the theme.

We like to be told these things.
We need to be reminded.

He sounds like a sort of priest.
What was your priesthood doing?

Nonsensical things, like spinning
a shallow great bowl of words
poised on the stick of a question,
pointing it this way and that

for an answering flash, as the bend
of a river may come in a flash
over miles and miles
from a fold in the hills, over miles.

We paid them no attention.

TO THOM GUNN IN LOS ALTOS, CALIFORNIA

Conquistador! Live dangerously, my Byron,
In this metropolis
Of Finistère. Drop off
The edge repeatedly, and come
Back to tell us! Dogs and cherry-trees
Are not your element although
You like them well enough when, cast
Ashore and briefly beached, our Commodore,
You take a turn among them, your cigar
Fragrant along a sunny garden wall,
Home between voyages, with your aunts in Kent.

Home . . . Is that home? Is even Land's End 'home'?
You shrug and say we are mid-Atlantic people,
You and I. I'd say for you
The mid-Pacific rather: somewhere out
On the International Dateline, so far out
Midsummer Oregon and midwinter Chile
Are equidistant, and 'the slow
Pacific swell' you generate lifts and crunches
Under the opalescent high fog with as much
Patience in one hemisphere as the other,
An exhalation from the depths you sound to.

The plesiosaur! Your lead-line has gone down to
The Age of Reptiles, even as
Over your head the flying lizard
Sprung from its Lompoc silo, Vandenberg Airforce Base,
Tracks high across mid-ocean to its target.
Ignore it, though a tidal wave will rage
From where it plunges, flood Japan
And poison Asia. This is the pacific
Ocean, the peacemaker. Nothing rhymes with this
Lethal indifference that you plumbed to even
Once in a bath-house in Sonoma County.

This is the end of the world. At the end, at the edge
We live among those for whom

As is natural enough
The edge is the navel of earth, and the end, the beginning.
Hope springs not eternal nor everywhere—does it
Spring in Kent? For these our friends, however,
It springs, it springs. Have we a share in it?
This is the Garden of Eden, the serpent coiled
Inside it is sleepy, reposeful. It need not flex
A muscle to take us. What are we doing here?
What am I doing, I who am scared of edges?

SEUR, NEAR BLOIS

That a toss of wheat-ears lapping
Church-walls should placate us
Is easy to understand
In the abstract. That in fact
The instance of seeing also
A well with its wrought-iron stanchion,
Of feeling a balmy coolness,
Of hearing a Sunday noon silence,
Of smelling the six ragged lime-trees,
A church-door avenue, should
Placate, compose, is as much
As to say that the eye and the nose,
Also the ear and the very
Surface of one's skin is
An ethical organ; and further,
If indeed it is further
Or even other, a learned
Historian of man's culture.

THREE POEMS OF SICILY

(1) The Fountain of Arethusa

    'Arethusa arose
    From her couch of snows
In the Akrokeraunian mountains . . .'
    More thrilling today
    My mother's way
With Shelley, than this fountain's
    Circus of grey
    Mullet, or sway
Of papyrus fronds. Pulsations
    Still rill it through;
    What once she knew
Of crags, reverberations,
    Couches of snows,
    The nymph still knows,
Still pushing her liquid lever
    Up and out,
    As when it brought
Greeks once in a choleric fever
    To Syracuse.
    Mother, my Muse,
These are the springs that matter:
    Small thrills sustain
    The source, not vain
Glories or consonants' clatter
    Down a moraine
    In Shelley's brain
Or his ear. Yet I hear it! One day
    In a parlour-game,
    Required to name
Mountains beginning with A,
    Proudly, aged ten,
    I pronounced it then:
The Akrokeraunian Mountains!
    Grown-ups demurred;
    But undeterred
Now as then I drink at those fountains!

(2) Syracuse

The one in the poem is not
The one that you will visit.
The city you may visit,
The poem also—one
Casts no light on the other.

Through the one there strays
One and one only walker;
The city exerts its claim
Upon the one who can
Meet it in curious ways.

By a brilliant turn of phrase?
No. For it is the past
Is brilliant, Pasternak says;
The debt we owe it, only
More modest coin repays.

So in the verdant, man-made
Latomìa, a grotto
Loud with seepage houses
No lonely inscrutable Tristan
And Iseult, but a rope-walk.

Rope-makers gone from under
Mottled impendings, still
Their hempen gossamers ran
Taut and knee-high through the shafted
Light and the cavernous air.

Gratitude, need, and gladness—
These are the names of the walker,
These are the strands of the hemp:
Gladness at meeting the need
The gratitude imposes.

This is our walker's scope.
You think he makes too bold?

To pay this visit, think
Of how to test a rope:
Swing on it, trust it to hold.

A gimcrack drum with spikes,
Knee-high, the T-shaped stretchers . . .
This is the phrase he will use:
Warm honesties of makeshift
Transvalue Syracuse.

(3) The Fountain of Cyane

Modesty, he kept saying,
Temperate, temperate . . . Yes,
The papyrus were swaying
Hardly at all, and late,
Late in the season the rings
Widened upon the reedy
Pool, and the beady-eyed frogs
Volleyed out after mayfly.

Fountain? No jet, no spume,
Spew nor spurt . . . Was this
Where Pluto's chariot hurtled
Up out of 'gloomy Dis'?
Male contumely, for that
First most seminal rape,
Proserpine's, prescribes
Some more vertiginous landscape.

Late, late in that season . . .
Easy, easy the lap
And rustle of blue waters . . .
Wholly a female occasion
This, as Demeter launches
One fish in a silver arc
To signalize her daughter's
Re-entry to the dark.

GEMONA-DEL-FRIULI, 1961-1976

We have written to Giulia, saying
'Are you still alive?'
And no reply comes.
This is a bad look out.

What sort of a life this is
I thought I knew, or I learned,
Some 15 years ago
Precisely in Giulia's country:

Gemona, the heartland, the forests
Living in an orange light
After calamity. That one!
That was the place;

Where a calamity, not
In any case undeserved,
Chastened, I thought, and instructed
Gravely, biddable me

As to the proper proportions
Of the dead to the living, of death
To life, and out of all
Proportion, love . . . Now this!

Earthquake! And the entire
Small city of Gemona
Flat in one enormous
Stir of that rock-ribbed earth

Which had not in 700
Years—for some of Gemona
Had stood that long—not stirred
Like that in 700 years.

What colour of justification,
What nice, austere proportion
Now can be put on the mountains?
At whose hands this chastisement?

AN APPARITION

Gina, I saw you walk
Suddenly, in white
Brassiere and panties under
A fish-net wrap; your sallow skin,

Firm and sullen to fire,
Inflamed the Panamanian
Day to exceptional ardours
In Tehuantepec Bay

As our Edwardian prow
Ploughed southward, and decrepit
Bodies basked in renewed
Delusory bronze and vigour.

The posh ships, P. & O.,
Trace in phosphorescent
Peppermint-fire on the oceans
An after-image of Empire.

The sun stooped down to take you,
Stiff on your bed in Boulder,
Colorado, Gina;
You will never grow older,

Nor will your empire ever,
Italo-American girl,
Crumble in Eritrea,
Dear wraith, raped by Apollo.

HORAE CANONICAE

PRIME

New every morning is the love
Our wakening and uprising prove,
Bond it in warranty a hundred proof.
Giving his thanks for roof, for bed and board,
Mr Saint Keble, meek and lowly,
White with rite, and clean with holy,
Wordplays to the morning's Lord.

TERCE

New every moment is the power
That activates us, active though we are . . .
At 9 o'clock, the scriptural 3rd hour,
Mr Saint William Law is eating his
Sweet humble pie: 'We have no more
Power of our own to move a hand or stir
A foot, than to stop clouds, or move the sun.'

SEXT

'Filling us with such bowels of
Compassion as when' (Come, Mr Law, we are furnished
With bowels, and they are full, or they are not;
What room for other organs?), glimpsing her
Appallingly in Cambridge Circus, tracing
The faceless angel who mounted her once and vanished,
'We see the miseries of an hospital.'

NONES

At 3 o'clock in the afternoon,
Loggy with gin, with wine, with Mexican beer,
Resignation to the will of God
Comes easy. That it should be 'hardly worth
Living in a world so full of changes
And revolutions'—ah, how wrong! Yet dozing,
Fanned in a garden-chair, is hardly 'prayer'.

VESPERS

This one for the telling of sins. And for
The original horror, the victimization, no problem.
But for our own, our particular own, in the sorry
Unrollings, where was the harm? Not nowhere, but
Where? In prayer, no place for 'all-over-the-place',
It comes to seem . . . My instructors' awful calm
Tell-tales the stink: half spunk, half frightened sweat.

COMPLINE

Now I lay me down to sleep
Perhaps not to wake, and I am alone in the house!
How much alone in whatever house of bone,
Suddenly I love my fellow creatures
So much, though for that the hour was Sext, was noon.
I tell you over feverishly, my loved ones,
You are my own, you are? My own! My own?

MORNING

Rose late: the jarring and whining
Of the parked cars under my windows, their batteries drained,
Somehow was spared. When I let out our schoolboy
Into the street, it was light: the place was alive and scented.

Spared too, for the most part, the puzzling tremulousness
That afflicts me often, these mornings. (I think
Either I need, so early, the day's first drink or
This is what a sense of sin amounts to:
Aghast incredulity at the continued success
Of an impersonation, the front put on to the world,
The responsibilities . . .)
                              Let all that go:
Better things throng these nondescript, barged-through streets
(The sun! The February sun, so happily far and hazy . . .)
Than a mill of ideas.
                         Sin, I will say, comes awake
With all the other energies, even at last the spark
Leaps on the sluggard battery, and one should have
Prosopopoeia everywhere: Stout Labour
Gets up with his pipe in his mouth or lighting
The day's first *Gauloise-filtre*; then stout
Caffein like a fierce masseur
Rams him abreast of the day; stout Sin
Is properly a-tremble; stout
Vociferous Electricity chokes and chokes,
Stumbles at last into coughings, and will soon
Come to the door with a telegram—'Operation
Some Day This Week'; and stout
Love gets up out of rumpled sheets and goes singing
Under his breath to the supermarket, the classroom,
The briskly unhooded
Bureaucratic typewriter. See how
Sol winks upon its clever keys, and Flora
In a northern winter, far underground,
Feels herself sore at nubs and nipples.

And that mob of ideas? Don't knock them. The sick pell-mell
Goes by the handsome Olympian name of Reason.

TO A TEACHER OF FRENCH

Sir, you were a credit to whatever
Ungrateful slate-blue skies west of the Severn
Hounded you out to us. With white, cropped head,
Small and composed, and clean as a Descartes
From as it might be Dowlais, 'Fiery' Evans
We knew you as. You drilled and tightly lipped
Le futur parfait dans le passé like
The Welsh Guards in St James's, your pretence
Of smouldering rage an able sergeant-major's.

We jumped to it all right whenever each
Taut smiling question fixed us. Then it came:
Crash! The ferrule smashed down on the first
Desk of the file. You whispered: *Quelle bêtise!*
Ecoutez, s'il vous plait, de quelle bêtise
On est capable!
                    Yet you never spoke
To us of poetry; it was purely language,
The lovely logic of its tenses and
Its accidence that, mutilated, moved you
To rage or outrage that I think was not
At all times simulated. It would never
Do in our days, dominie, to lose
Or seem to lose your temper. And besides
Grammarians are a dying kind, the day
Of histrionic pedagogy's over.

You never taught me Ronsard, no one did,
But you gave me his language. He addressed
The man who taught him Greek as *Toi qui dores*
(His name was Jean Dorat) *la France de l'or.*
I couldn't turn a phrase like that on 'Evans';
And yet you gild or burnish something as,
At fifty in the humidity of Touraine,
Time and again I profit by your angers.

WIDOWERS

'i segni dell' antica fiamma'

Atheist, Laodicean or
Whatever name our hand-to-mouth evasions
Earn for us, all of us have the thought
That states of soul in some uncertain sort
Survive us—sealed, it could be, in locations:
A yard, a coomb, an inn, a Cornish tor.

These leak their fragrances. To tap the fount
Of consolation calls on us for no
Dexterity at first; it isn't hard
To bruise a hip by falling in that yard
Or on that hillside. Hurt is all we know,
Stout alpenstock as we begin to mount

The purgatorial steeps, the terraces
Kicked back behind us. Then we sweat, we stink,
We fear that we forget. Our ancient haunts
Glow far above us, and the glimmer taunts
Our coming numbness. There she dwells, we think . . .
She does, although our need to think so passes.

SOME SHIRES REVISITED

(1) NORFOLK

The scroll is defaced; the worm
Is in the roof; and the flaking
Inscription may be cleared
Of ivy but, if it is read,
It must be on the firm
Presumption it is mistaken.

Reading from haunted air
Certain great (which is not to say, good)
Historical presences—Walpole,
Nelson, landmarks in Norfolk—
I had readers who thought that I could
Never in fact have been there.

(2) DEVONSHIRE

'Into Spooner's, looking for remnants,'
Said Mrs John; and her face was wistful
As if the town she recalled, the tenements
Burnt in the blitz, the streets like tunnels
Turning and twisting at cliff-like corners
Under the web of the wires, were a haven
Unspeakably lovely and calm. The destroyers
Had threatened her future; the young rebuilders
Tore down that future perfect in the past
Of a new-planned Plymouth, 1951.

(3) LEICESTERSHIRE

Clinton-Baddeley, Richards,
Blunden . . . these I have blessed:
Three good men named, and as many
Of those who invited them there
Unnamed, their equals or betters,
Upholders of what they professed
To care for, the world of letters
In the not quite wholly benighted
Midlands of England. In these
Worthies I have delighted
With a droll rhyme or two;
Leicestershire, when it housed them,
Did better than it knew.

(4) STAFFORDSHIRE

for Charles Tomlinson

'As once on Thracian Hebrus side' (to use
Your own Etrurian idiom, jasper-ware)

    'The tree-enchanter Orpheus fell
    By Bacchanalians torn',

So I have seen you—gasping, bloodied—fall
Time and again over twenty-five years, and the Maenads

Quite honestly astonished: 'But we surely
(Serenely, suavely) always gave him his due?'

Your love of our country has not been returned, and won't be.

(5) BEDFORDSHIRE

Crop-headed nonconformists,
   Cromwell's Ironsides, sprang
Out of this clay. But not all
   The sour battalions rang
With benedictions when
   The sage dictator willed
   A king was to be killed.

Redbrick, round-windowed chapels,
   Squat on these gravels, rose,
And yet not all their broadcloth,
   When the time came, chose
The Red Flag as the only
   Colours to march to. Some
   Never came back from the Somme.

Born one of them, I think
   How it might be to be French;
How Protestants might man
   Pétain's untenable trench
And, rendering unto Caesar
   What's due to Caesar, might
   Die fighting the wrong good fight.

GRUDGING RESPECT

As when a ruined face
Lifted among those crowding
For the young squire's largesse
Perceives him recognize
Her and she grabs, not for any
Languidly lofted penny
They scrabble for, but for his eyes
And pockets them, their clouding
That instant; and the abruptness
With which his obliging is checked,
His suddenly leaving the place . . .

Just so may a grudging respect
Be, from a despised one,
Not just better than none
At all, but sweeter than any.

A SPRING SONG

'stooped to truth and moralized his song'

Spring pricks a little. I get out the maps.
Time to demoralize my song, high time.
Vernal a little. *Primavera*. First
Green, first truth and last.
High time, high time.

A high old time we had of it last summer?
I overstate. But getting out the maps . . .
Look! Up the valley of the Brenne,
Louise de la Vallière . . . Syntax collapses.
High time for that, high time.

To Château-Renault, the tannery town whose marquis
Rooke and James Butler whipped in Vigo Bay
Or so the song says, an amoral song
Like Ronsard's where we go today
Perhaps, perhaps tomorrow.

Tomorrow and tomorrow and . . . Get well!
Philip's black-sailed familiar, avaunt
Or some word as ridiculous, the whole
Diction kit begins to fall apart.
High time it did, high time.

High time and a long time yet, my love!
Get out that blessed map.
Ageing, you take your glasses off to read it.
Stooping to truth, we potter to Montoire.
High time, my love. High time and a long time yet.

A WISTFUL POEM CALLED 'READERS'

Oh (they will say) how funny of him! I mean,
What a peculiar thing for him to do.
If it's a love-poem, why is it all about France?
I just don't see the relevance, do you?

Who's Marquis Rooke and Mrs Valley? Brenne
(Gun understood) would make a sort of sense.
Or is it all that Eliot thingumajig,
A—*you know*, what's-it—'pseudo-reference'?

I just don't get the point about the horse,
Do you? The horse? Why, *there*, the Vigo bay . . .
He's always on about horses, this one is;
They're a sort of obsession with him, wouldn't you say?

What? Oh I see, like *Turkish*! But I thought
That sort of bey, you wrote it with an E.
We *have* to assume the man knows how to spell!
Now, more to the point, what's this about the sea?

The sea? Well, black-*sailed*, silly! Oh I say,
You're coming on—that's very good indeed:
Spanish Armada. 'Philip's' clinches it.
Of course! At last, we really have a lead.

And yet I'd say his imagery wasn't,
Well, you know, *integrated*. Here's perhaps
(Okay, *perhaps*) a horse; and there's the sea;
And, somewhere, Love; and then all this about maps . . .

It doesn't add up, is what I mean. Okay.
OKAY (Don't shout!), suppose we do take 'bey'
In your sense, as a sort of pun (I know,
Empson and that), still, what does he mean to *say*?

And anyhow who wants a sort of sheikh
In the middle of France, if we need to have France at all
Which I take leave to doubt. Take *leave*, I said.
What do you mean, that's funny? It's perfectly normal.

'Stooped to truth . . .' Who did? And how'd he do it?
Mostly, I mean, you'd think Truth was above us.
The sort of acrobatics that this poet
Is good at, we can do without, Lord love us!

TOWNEND, 1976

When does a town become a city? This
That ends where I begin it, at Townend
With Wright the Chemist (one of the few not changed),
Grows cityfied, though still my drab old friend.

Thanks therefore for the practical piety
Of E. G. Tasker, antiquarian;
His *Barnsley Streets*. Unshed, my tears hang heavy
Upon the high-gloss pages where I scan

What else, though, but remembered homely squalor?
Generations of it! Eldon Street
Smells of bad drains of forty years ago
Ah sweetly. But should penury smell sweet?

An end to it then. An end to that town. Townend.
A Tetley's house, the Wheatsheaf, holds its station
Since 1853, where Dodworth Road
Stars into five streets, 'major intersection'.

Portentous words! Hoist up to suit South Yorkshire's
Administrative centre, such perforce
This town must live with, must live up or down to:
'Intersection'; 'shopping precinct'; 'concourse' . . .

And not to be sneered nor sniffed at. This is not,
It never was, Blackheath or Tunbridge Wells;
No buildings 'listed', nor deserving it,
Press to be saved as civic ardour swells.

Of cities much is written. Even Scripture
Has much to say of them, though mostly under
The inauspicious name of 'Babylon'.
What a town is, one is left to wonder.

Is homely squalor, then, its sign and function?
Is it a swollen village? If it is,
Are swellings lanced? Have towns a size or shape
More than villages and less than cities?

I think of the Irish, or perhaps the Celtic
'Townland'. (Also, 'township' might provoke us.)
'Townland', so my Irish years persuade me,
Means never a star of roads, never a focus:

Never! By no means! There's a lead at last:
Focus, a hearth. The English circumstance
In town or village draws to a hearth, a fug:
Townend, the up-draught up five flues at once!

Whatever meets that need, it's certain 'concourse',
'Complex' nor 'intersection' ever could.
Upon their hunkers, 'carring' (cowering) down
By a spent flame, the colliers of my boyhood . . .

That was in the 'thirties, 'the Depression';
Outside whatever pub it is in Kingstone,
Unwanted in the open, nipping air,
All the one class, a hardship town, all one.

Something, I take it, not to be found in cities;
No, nor in villages, what with parson, squire,
Farmer and farm-hand. (Just as well: the once
And ever martyred stoke a sullen fire.)

Up above Glossop, weeping cloud at Woodhead;
Up again after, over the last high hogsback,
The clean black waters shine up steel, not silver,
The peat is black, the lowering skies are black.

Millicent Dillon, if you ever visit
This town as you say you will, this is the way:
Ashbourne to Buxton, Buxton to Glossop, over
To an ash-boled England and a Baltic day.

For this is under us now, as we come down:
The Silkstone seam, where woods compacted lay
Shade upon shade, multiplication of blackness
That seeps up through: 'black Barnsley', we would say.

The sneer of it—black Barnsley, that my mother
Indignantly thought corrupted out of 'bleak',
'Bleak Barnsley'. Who else cared? Corruption in
All that we do, decay in all we speak.

Ireland, America, the Atlantic writ
Here runs no longer. Out of the sunset shires,
Ireland, and Wales, they called us; and we shut
Behind us the West that beckons, that aspires.

Westward, the moors: shield more than barrier, closing
Utopias off. We were not to be tricked:
Depravity stalked the streets with us. A city
Needs, on the contrary, a red-light district.

Barracks, industrial barracks: 'town'
In that late sense. Sensational the feat,
Making a city of the regimental
Lines, as you might say: Day Street, Peel Street, Pitt Street!

Well, it has started; air is let in, and light,
All to the good. And now what will befall?
Concourse and complex, underpass and precinct,
The scale not human but angelical:

Squalor on that scale; homeliness as 'home'
Might be for Rebel Angels, or their hordes,
Machinists of 'machines for living in';
No fug upon the windy drawing-boards!

Some things get better: not *in situ*, in
Stone (that gets worse), or steel; but in
Our knowing, though our architect were Wren,
We live in Babylon, we aspire in sin.

The end of a town—however mean, however
Much of a byword—marks the end of an age,
An age of worn humility. Hereafter,
The Prince of Darkness and his equipage!